Watching
Desert Wildlife
by Jim Arnosky

NATIONAL GEOGRAPHIC SOCIETY

Washington, D.C.

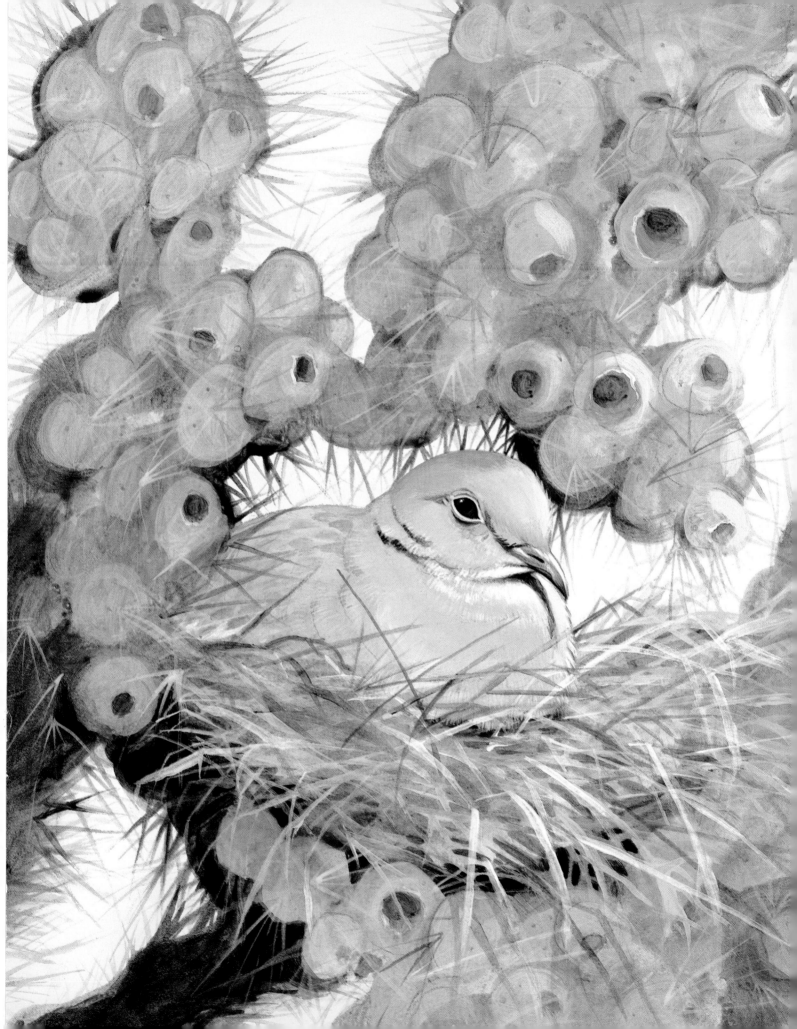

Introduction

For years the desert has beckoned to me with a challenge to discover new places and see different animals. This year my wife, Deanna, and I went to see the Chihuahuan Desert in Texas and New Mexico, and the Sonoran Desert in Arizona. We drove all the way, slowly, to fully appreciate the vastness of the land.

We walked many desert trails and everywhere we went, we saw wildlife. We saw lizards scooting along fence rails and sunning themselves on warm, trail-side boulders. We saw snakes slithering across dusty desert roads. Deanna spotted bighorn sheep on a Texas hillside. In Arizona I discovered a mourning dove nesting in a cactus.

While my naturalist's eye watched for glimpses of wildlife, my artist's eye noticed how rocks, not trees, dominated the landscape; colors vibrated through vaporless air; and water was nowhere to be seen, but locked inside every living thing.

Jim Arnosky
Ramtails 1998

Mourning dove nesting in a cholla cactus

Spotting Desert Birds

My first rule for finding wild animals and birds has always been: Find the watery places, and you will find wildlife. This was not so in the waterless landscape of the desert. However, I quickly learned that, just as in my familiar forested hills of Vermont, the secret to spotting birds in the desert was to look high, midway, and low in the scenery. This simple practice enabled me to see birds in all the places we visited. I spotted birds high atop boulder piles and in the middle branches of desert shrubs and trees. I spotted birds that were perched on the spiny arms of cactus plants, and birds walking or running on the stony ground.

Deanna and I saw turkeys marching slowly around the creosote bushes. We noted woodpeckers hammering dead trees and fallen branches. We watched grackles hop along the ledges of canyon walls. And occasionally, we heard the familiar sound of crows cawing as they flew overhead in the cloudless sky.

My favorite desert bird is the cactus wren. These robin-size birds are speckled birds, and speckled birds are great fun to paint. The first cactus wren I saw was perched on the very top of a 40-foot-high saguaro cactus. With my telephoto lens, I focused closely on the wren's long black toes. It was fascinating how the bird grasped the cactus spines with its toenails without its toes getting pierced. I soon learned this to be true with all the perching birds in the desert.

Purple martins and organ pipe cactus

Cactus wren

IN THE DESERT, LOOK UP HIGH, AT EYE LEVEL, AND LOW FOR BIRDS.

Common flicker

THIS BIRD WAS AT MY EYE LEVEL, PECKING AWAY ON A BROKEN BRANCH.

THE GAMBEL'S QUAIL IS SEEN MOST OFTEN ON THE GROUND.

Roadrunner

This desert bird is called a roadrunner because often it is seen running on the road. Roadrunners have long, strong legs for running and extra long tails for balance. A roadrunner's beak is large, heavy, and sharp. The beak is used to stab and kill insects, spiders, rodents, lizards, and snakes—all roadrunner food. The snakes roadrunners kill and eat are usually under 18 inches long. Since there are more than 30 species of rattlesnakes living where roadrunners live, a lot of the snakes roadrunners eat are rattlers.

For a roadrunner, killing a rattlesnake takes time. The bird hops all around the snake, forcing it to strike repeatedly. But a roadrunner makes a tricky target. Its legs are thin and armored with scales. Its body is mostly fluffed feathers. After missing strike after strike, the snake becomes exhausted. Then the roadrunner stabs its deadly beak at the rattler's soft skull.

I painted this roadrunner life-size. You can see that even this very young rattler would be a bellyful. Although roadrunners peck apart small prey, they swallow snakes whole.

Roadrunner shown life-size

Coral Snakes and Rattlesnakes

In the desert, a wildlife watcher also has to watch out for certain wildlife. There are spiders that bite and scorpions that sting. There are poisonous snakes—coral snakes and rattlesnakes.

The coral snake, with its colorful, candy-cane marking, is a usually slow-moving snake that crawls in and out of rocky crevices. Coiled tightly, a coral snake can fit into a surprisingly small space. The bite of a coral snake contains the same venom (poison) found in cobras. It attacks the nervous system and can be fatal. Coral snakes eat lizards and other small snakes.

Rattlesnake venom attacks the blood. Rattlesnakes are pit vipers. A pit viper has two large pits in its head, one between each eye and nostril. Inside the pits are heat-sensing organs that help rattlesnakes find warm-blooded prey in total darkness.

In the desert, we walked slowly, always stayed on established trails, and kept an eye out for snakes. In most of the places we visited, we saw no snakes. But we knew they were there, coiled and camouflaged in their favorite spots.

THERE ARE A NUMBER OF BANDED, NON-VENOMOUS SNAKES THAT RESEMBLE CORAL SNAKES. REMEMBER THIS OLD SAYING: RED TOUCHES YELLOW—DEADLY FELLOW.

Coral snake shown life-size

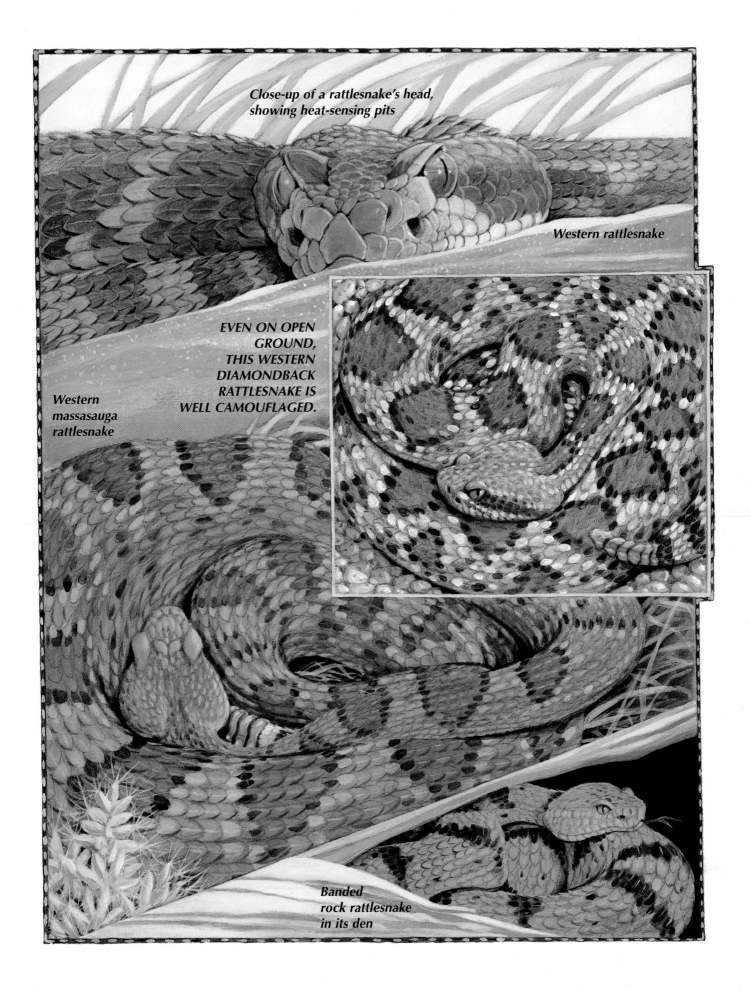

Close-up of a rattlesnake's head, showing heat-sensing pits

Western rattlesnake

EVEN ON OPEN GROUND, THIS WESTERN DIAMONDBACK RATTLESNAKE IS WELL CAMOUFLAGED.

Western massasauga rattlesnake

Banded rock rattlesnake in its den

Non-venomous Snakes

Not all the snakes in the desert are venomous. There are milk snakes, gopher snakes, king snakes, hognose snakes, and garter snakes—all non-venomous—living in deserts. Some, like the Sonoran whipsnake in my painting, are good climbers and may be seen not only on the ground, but coiled or draped on the branches of trees or shrubs. There is nothing to fear from these snakes as long as you let them be.

In the desert, where rattlesnake species outnumber all other species of snakes, the chances of a rattler sharing an area with non-venomous snakes are high. All snakes have the same needs. They need prey to hunt and eat, ground cover or rock crevices for hiding, and sunny spots where they can warm themselves.

Never approach a snake to see what kind it is. Even a harmless snake will strike and may bite if you step too closely. And as I said, in the desert the sight of one harmless snake could mean there are dangerous snakes in the area. Watch snakes the way you watch birds—with binoculars. When viewed this way, closely but from a safe distance, every snake you spot can be enjoyed as a beautiful wild creature. And the snake can go about its natural business, uninhibited by your interest.

Sonoran whipsnake shown life-size

Lizards

I was always watching the ground for lizards. I enjoyed spotting various lizard species on the trails we walked in parks and refuges, and in residential areas. I videotaped lizards whenever I had the chance. As often happens with wildlife, when we went looking for lizards, even in places they are known to be plentiful, we saw few or none. But when we were simply strolling along a path admiring the cactus blooms, we spotted lizards everywhere. Look for small lizards in broad daylight, sunning themselves or dashing across the ground. These tiny, speedy creatures are a pure delight to watch. Larger lizards can be seen in early morning and later in the day, in the hour before sunset. These are the coolest, most comfortable times of the desert day.

Of all the lizards on my wish list, I had hoped to see the horned lizard, but I saw none. Horned lizards are so completely camouflaged that they are the most difficult of all lizards to spot. I'm certain Deanna and I walked by one or two of them squatting flat against the ground, blending perfectly with the buff-colored rocks and pebbles.

SOME LIZARDS CAN BE IDENTIFIED BY SHAPE ALONE.

GECKOS HAVE A SOFT, MISSHAPEN LOOK.

SKINKS ARE SLENDER AND SMOOTHLY TAPERED FROM NOSE TO TAIL.

WHIPTAILS HAVE VERY LONG, WHIPLIKE TAILS THAT MAKE UP ONE-THIRD THE LIZARD'S TOTAL LENGTH.

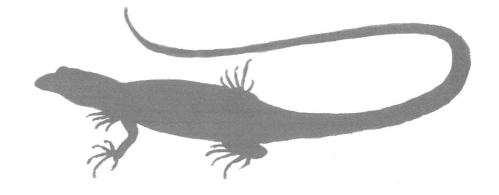

MOST NORTH AMERICAN SPECIES OF LIZARDS ARE IN THE IGUANID FAMILY. THE LIZARDS ON THIS PAGE ARE IGUANIDS.

Earless lizard

Spiny lizard

Horned lizard

Collared lizard

Chuckwalla

Gila Monster

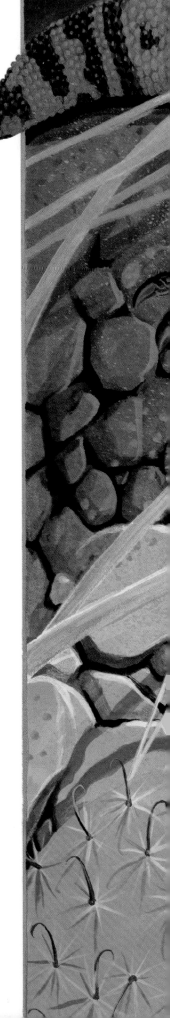

There are only two venomous lizards in the world, and both are native to North America. One is the Mexican beaded lizard. The other is the Gila monster, which lives in the deserts of the southwestern United States. The Gila monster is a beaded lizard. The beads are rounded scales.

Because Gila monsters are large and brightly colored, they should be easy to spot. But at dusk, when they are most active, their colors look darker and blend into the scenery.

Gila monsters spend much of the day underground in their tunnels. They have strong, wide claws for digging in the dry, hard desert soil. A thick, stubby tail stores water and fat, which can sustain the lizard when food becomes scarce.

Gila monsters eat bird eggs, insects, snakes, rodents, and other lizards. When large prey is caught, the Gila monster bites tightly and holds on so its venom, which is secreted from glands in the jaws, can seep into the victim's bite wound. This takes some time. Gila monsters do everything rather slowly except bite. They strike with surprising speed. These are very dangerous animals that must be watched out for and never approached closely. When a Gila monster does bite a person, it instinctively clamps on to slowly inject its venom. It may even hold on until pried loose by the doctor treating the bite! Gila monster bites are not common and, though serious and extremely painful, are rarely fatal.

Gila monsters are non-aggressive by nature. If left unmolested and given their space, they can be watched and enjoyed like any other lizard.

Gila monster shown life-size

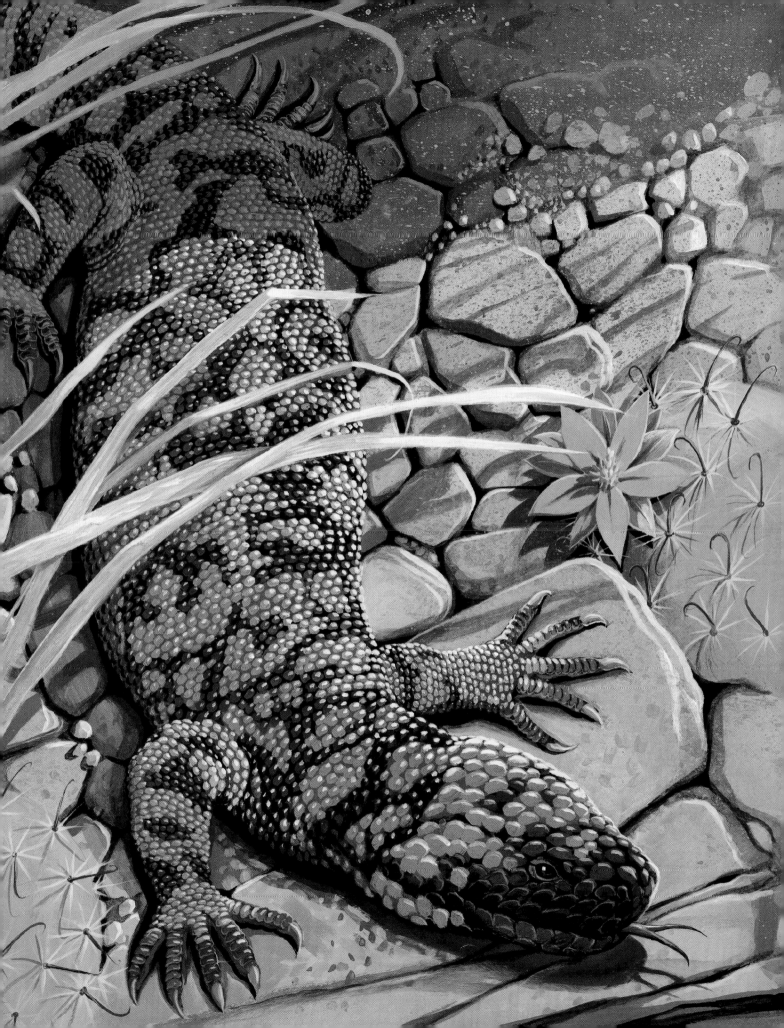

Desert Deer

I saw my first wild desert deer just north of Phoenix, Arizona. They were white-tailed deer resting on a knoll overgrown with cactus plants.

The white-tailed deer is the most widely distributed deer, found in nearly every state. It is named for the white hair on the underside of its tail. The deer on the hill looked like Coues (pronounced COWS) white-tails. The Coues deer is a subspecies of white-tailed deer that lives exclusively in the southwestern deserts. They are rather small deer. An adult Coues deer would look like a yearling in a herd of Texas, Virginia, or Vermont white-tailed deer.

The other deer inhabiting our deserts is the mule deer, which is found throughout the West. Mule deer are bigger and heavier than white-tailed deer, and their antlers differ from those of white-tailed deer in that they grow forked tines (or points). White-tailed deer antlers grow single tines. Mule deer have small white tails with black tips, and their ears are extra large. That's where they get their name.

I've been a deer seeker my whole life. I've looked for them in forests, fields, savannas, swamps, even on coastal islands. Yet, I wasn't looking for them in the desert. My mind was geared toward lizards, snakes, and birds. But the deer on that cactus-covered hill were a surprise. They were such a familiar animal to me, they made me a little homesick. For the first time on our desert trip, I realized how far we had traveled.

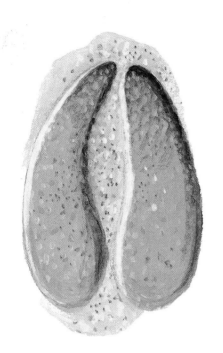

DESERT DEER HOOVES BECOME ROUNDED AT THE TIPS FROM WEARING AGAINST ROCKS AND DRY, GRAVELLY GROUND.

THESE ARE TRACK SIZE AND SHAPE COMPARISONS FOR WHITE-TAILED DEER AND OTHER DESERT-DWELLING HOOFED ANIMALS.

White-tailed deer *Mule deer* *Peccary (a kind of wild pig)* *Bighorn sheep* *Pronghorn*

Coues deer

White-tailed deer

Mule deer

Pronghorn

We were traveling on a highway through the high plateau desert of western New Mexico. On both sides of the road the landscape of blonde grasses dotted with dark creosote bushes stretched flat for miles. Deanna was driving. I was making notes on the terrain. Then I spotted them—a whole herd of pronghorns resting by a waterhole. The waterhole was stained deep pink by the red soil. The pink water sparkled.

There were many males in the herd. They had the "pronged" horns. The females had smaller, prongless spikes. Most of the herd was obscured by the dust they were kicking up. All I could see were brilliant white throat patches and black horns. I'll never forget the scene: the pink pool; the pronghorns moving about, red-brown and white against the blonde desert grass; and clouds of dust rising into the air—the only clouds in the blue, dry sky.

Birds of Prey

A long car trip is ideal for spotting and watching birds of prey. In the vast expanse of western Texas, where you can see the Rio Grande in the distance as a shimmering blue line, we counted hawk after hawk perched along the roadside. I even caught a glimpse of a few falcons. One of them, I believe, was an Aplomado falcon—rare in the U.S., but we were close to the border of Mexico where this small, beautiful falcon is more common.

In the desert, hawks and falcons feed on lizards, snakes, other birds, and small rodents. So wherever you see a hawk, you know there are many small animals in the area. One hawk every two or three miles indicates large populations of prey species.

Turkey vultures soared high over the desert, smelling the rising hot air for the scent of death. Vultures depend entirely on carrion (dead animals) for sustenance. I saw an eerie looking sextet of vultures all standing hunched over the remains of some large, unfortunate desert creature.

Another carrion feeder is the crested caracara, a Mexican eagle that often crosses the border. Caracaras can sometimes be spotted mingling with vultures. Like vultures, caracaras are more often seen in flight or standing on the ground, rather than perched on a branch.

YOU CAN TELL WHAT KIND OF BIRD OF PREY IS FLYING OVERHEAD BY ITS SILHOUETTE.

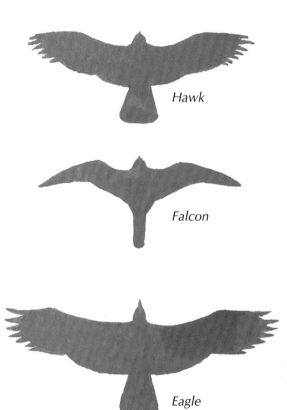

Hawk

Falcon

Eagle

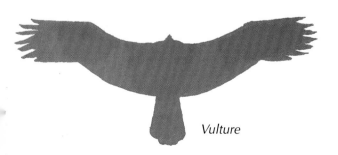

Vulture

BIRDS OF PREY CAN BE IDENTIFIED BY BEAK SHAPE.

VULTURES HAVE LONG, NARROW BEAKS.

THE TURKEY VULTURE'S BALD HEAD IS AN IDENTIFYING FEATURE.

Red-tailed hawk

ANY LARGE BIRD YOU SEE PERCHED ON THE TOP OF A TREE, CACTUS, OR YUCCA PLANT MOST LIKELY IS A HAWK.

Harris' hawk

HAWKS AND FALCONS HAVE SMALL, SHARPLY CURVED BEAKS.

EAGLES HAVE LARGE, HEAVY, HOOKED BEAKS.

Crested caracara

Elf Owl

In the Sonoran Desert, every time I saw a hole in a giant saguaro cactus, I wondered what was living inside. Most saguaro holes are originally excavated by woodpeckers as nest holes. After the woodpeckers raise their young, they leave the cactus. The abandoned holes provide homes for other birds, including one of the smallest birds of prey—the elf owl.

Measuring only six inches from the top of its head to the tip of its tail, the elf owl is the smallest of all owls. It is so small, it feeds mostly on insects and young scorpions. Elf owls occasionally do eat little lizards and even mice, but these are big, strong prey for such a small owl to catch and kill.

The life-size elf owl in the painting has caught a sphynx moth. Big fat sphynx moths are a favorite food of elf owls, and the owls must compete for them and for crunchy scorpions with the many species of desert bats.

Elf owls have a high-pitched *kew* call and make other whistling and whinnying sounds. When you hear strange whistles, whinnies, or a distinctive *kew kew kew* in the desert night, you will know a tiny owl lives nearby.

Long ago in the mountains of Pennsylvania, I used to stand in the evenings on our cabin porch and listen for the calls of another small owl—the screech owl. Sometimes by imitating the calls, I could lure an owl closer to the cabin. Once, one landed on the top wrung of a wooden ladder standing right beside the porch! I wonder if elf owls would do the same? If you live in the desert and have an elf owl as a neighbor, try calling it in. Let me know if it comes.

Desert Squirrels

One bright Arizona afternoon, I saw a tiny squirrel dash across a baseball field as if it were part of the game, stealing a base—safe! It disappeared down a hole.

It was an antelope squirrel.

Antelope squirrels are beautiful little creatures. They remind me of chipmunks, only they are smaller and more sleek. Antelope squirrels live in burrows. They can be seen on stone walls, in the low branches of trees, and even on prickly cactus plants, which they carefully climb to eat cactus fruit. Antelope squirrels gather food in their cheeks and carry it off to their burrows for storage, like chipmunks do.

The largest desert squirrel is the rock squirrel. I saw more of these than of any other squirrel species. A rock squirrel looks like a gray squirrel with chalky white bands down its back. Many of the rock squirrels we saw were in parks and on public walks, tempting people to feed them. I loved watching these bold, fearless squirrels, but I never fed them. Fearless squirrels can become aggressive and bite, and some carry diseases that can infect people.

Rock squirrels also live in much wilder places, from low deserts to high canyonlands. On the South Rim of the Grand Canyon, I watched a rock squirrel sprawl lazily on its belly and, resting its chin on the canyon rim, gaze contentedly into the abyss.

I SPOTTED THIS ROCK SQUIRREL PERCHED ATOP A ROCK PILE ON A HILLSIDE OVERLOOKING THE CITY OF PHOENIX.

MOST OF THE SQUIRRELS YOU SEE IN THE DESERT ARE GROUND-DWELLING SQUIRRELS.

Harris' antelope squirrel

White-tailed antelope squirrel

Rock squirrel

ANTELOPE SQUIRRELS RUN WITH THEIR TAILS UP.

PRAIRIE DOGS ARE GROUND SQUIRRELS THAT LIVE IN GRASSLANDS AND DESERTS.

Hummingbirds

Where I live in the East, we have only one species of hummingbird: the ruby-throated hummingbird. Out West there are many more species of "hummers." The deserts of the Southwest are a hummingbird watchers' paradise. There are resident species, and there are species that pass through on their migrations to and from Mexico.

We were able to enjoy many of the desert's hummingbirds. It was spring and the desert was in bloom. We found hummers around wildflowers and cactuses blooming high in a canyon, down along a dry river bed, and in the desert lowlands.

Hummingbirds are very protective of their favorite feeding spots. They will confront and chase other hummingbirds that compete with them for the flower nectar and small insects they thrive on. Getting all it can eat is important to a bird that, each day, burns five times as many calories as a full-grown person!

You can use up a lot of energy just trying to see a hummingbird clearly. Its powerful little wings zip it this way and buzz it that way, as the tiny bird moves rapidly from flower to flower and plant to plant. Suddenly, it hovers in midair, and you try to freeze the image in your mind. Zip! The bird flies away before you can.

A HUMMINGBIRD OPENS ITS BILL TO SNAP UP INSECTS...

AND SLIPS ITS TONGUE THROUGH THE OPEN TIP OF ITS CLOSED BILL TO SIP NECTAR.

Male ♂
Female ♀

HERE ARE SIX SPECIES
OF HUMMINGBIRDS
YOU CAN LOOK FOR.

Broad-billed hummingbird
♀

*Broad-billed
hummingbird
with feet
dangling to
cool off*
♂

Calliope
hummingbird
♀

MOST FEMALE
HUMMINGBIRDS
ARE BUFF COLORED
ON THE BREAST
AND THROAT.

Calliope hummingbird ♂

Rivoli hummingbird ♂

Costa's hummingbird
♂

*Male black-chinned
hummingbird inserting
bill in a tubular flower*
♂

THE MALE'S
IRIDESCENT
THROAT PATCH
IS CALLED A
GORGET.

Allen's hummingbird ♂

A HUMMINGBIRD'S
GORGET LOOKS BLACK
IN CERTAIN LIGHTING.

I went to the desert to feel the heat of the desert sun and breathe the dry air. I went to the desert to see its wide open places. I went with my eyes open wide, watchful for snakes and scorpions, and alert, ready to see all the wonderful wild animals who make their homes amid the thorns and spines.

I came home from the desert with a fresh new outlook on nature and wildlife. I felt bigger and broader, happy in the knowledge that I had discovered another world.

Costa's hummingbirds

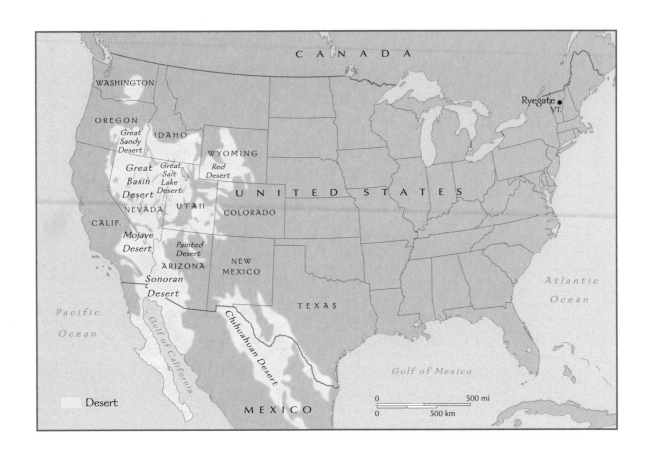

Inside the map:

C A N A D A

WASHINGTON

OREGON

Great Sandy Desert

IDAHO

WYOMING

Great Basin Desert

Great Salt Lake Desert

Red Desert

NEVADA

UTAH

COLORADO

U N I T E D S T A T E S

CALIF.

Mojave Desert

Painted Desert

ARIZONA

NEW MEXICO

Sonoran Desert

Chihuahuan Desert

TEXAS

Pacific Ocean

Gulf of California

Atlantic Ocean

Gulf of Mexico

MEXICO

Ryegate • VT.

Desert

0   500 mi
0   500 km

ALL OF THE DESERT AREAS IN THE LOWER 48 STATES, INCLUDING AN UNNAMED AREA IN WASHINGTON AND OREGON, ARE INCLUDED ON THIS MAP.

After a lifetime spent studying the plants and animals in the Northeast, particularly the many creatures that live near his home in Ryegate, Vermont, Jim Arnosky and his wife, Deanna, set out for the deserts of the Southwest. Most experts agree that a desert is an area of land that receives 10 inches or less of precipitation, such as rainfall, snow, or hail, a year. But though there is little water available, desert wildlife is rich and varied.

This book records Jim Arnosky's first-time, first-hand observations as he and Deanna visited parts of the Sonoran and Chihuahuan Deserts.

Jim Arnosky has won the *Washington Post*/Children's Book Guild Award for his overall contribution to nonfiction for children. He has also received the Eva L. Gordon Award for outstanding children's science literature, and the Christopher Award for *Drawing from Nature*, one of his many popular ALA Notable Books.